Secret Diary - A B[...]
180 Day Person[...]

MW00899097

For Beginners - Level 1 - Girls

My Name:

My Address:

Today's Date:

Date:_____

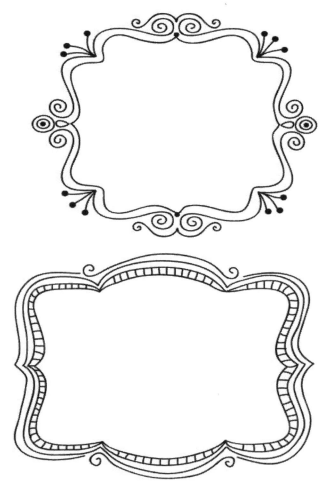

Date:_____

ii

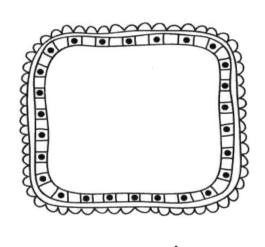

Date:_____

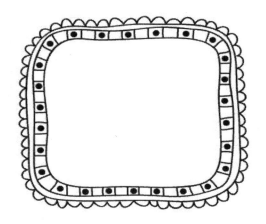

Date:_____

> "Believe you can
> and you're halfway there."
>
> — Theodore Roosevelt

Date:_____

Date:_____

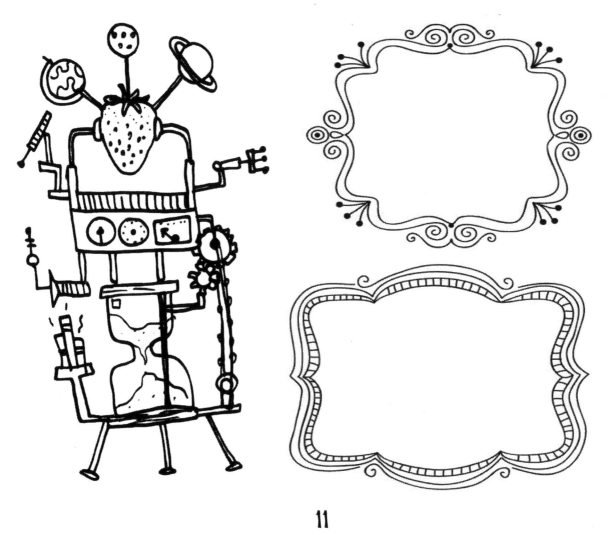

Date:_____

12

Date:_____

13

Date:_____

Date:_____

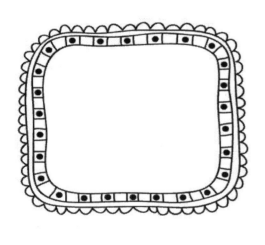

Date:_____

"If you want to change the world, pick up your pen and write."

– Martin Luther

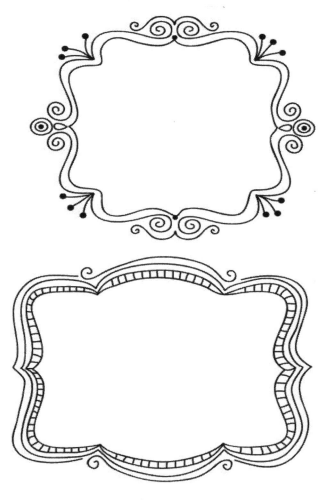

Date:_____

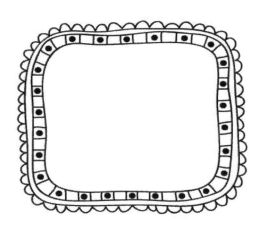

Date:_____

Date:_____

23

Date:_____

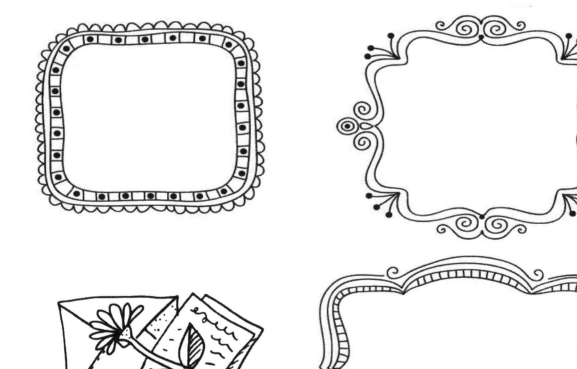

Date:_____

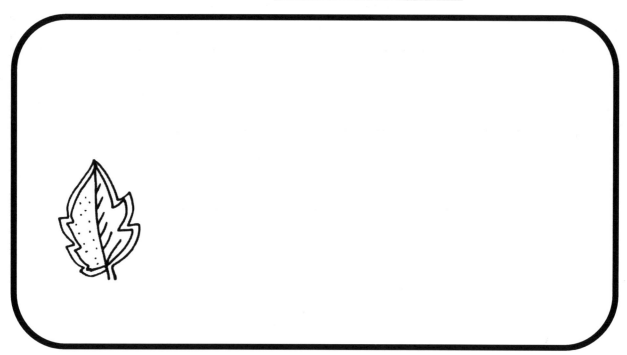

Date:_____

"Follow your dreams,
believe in yourself,
and don't give up."

— Rachel Corrie

Date:_____

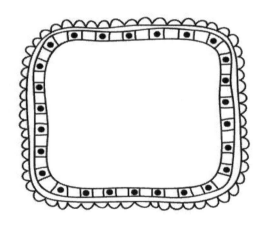

Date:_____

Date:_____

Date:_____

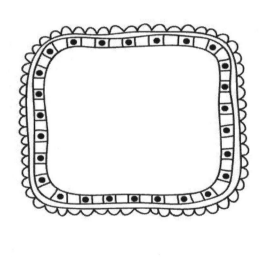

Date:_____

Date:_____

Date:_____

"Do what you can,
with what you've got,
where you are."

– Squire Bill Widener

Date:_____

Date:_____

Date:_____

Date:_____

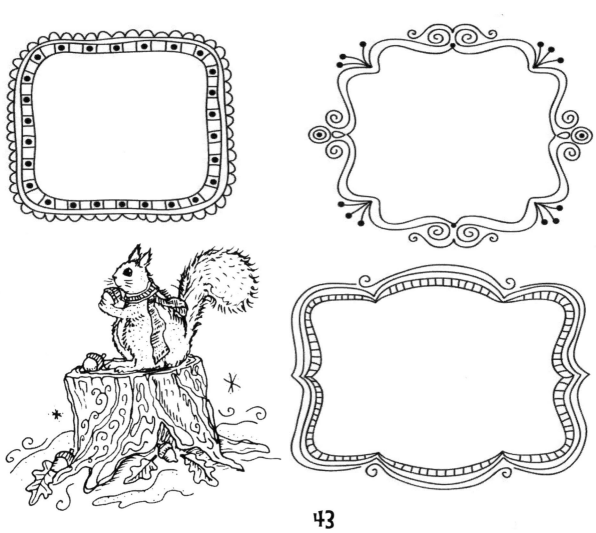

Date:_____

Date:_____

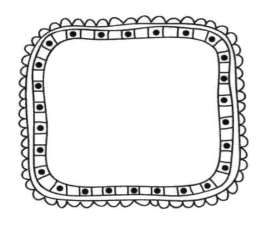

Date:_____

Date:_____

"Be the friend
you hope to have."

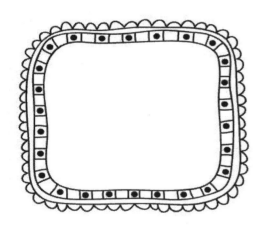

Date:_____

Date:_____

Date:_____

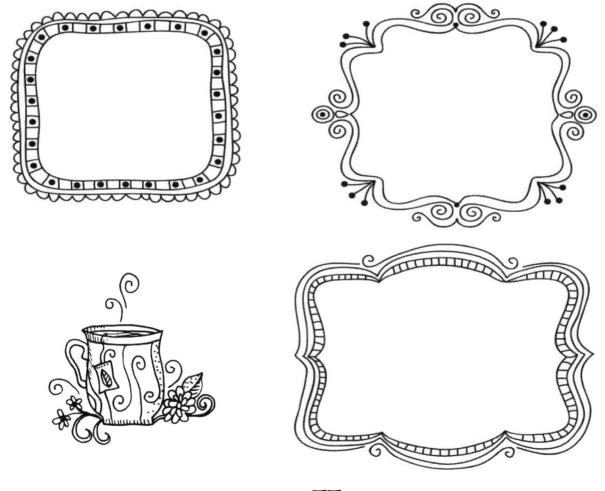

Date:_____

Date:_____

Date:_____

"As a man changes his own nature, so does the attitude of the world change towards him."

— Mahatma Gandhi

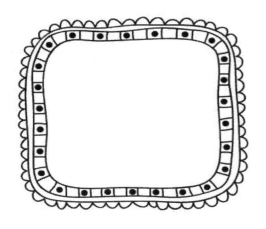

Date:_____

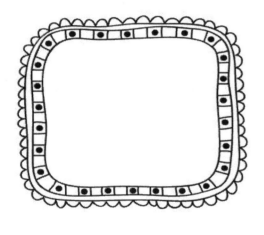

Date:_____

Date:_____

Date:_____

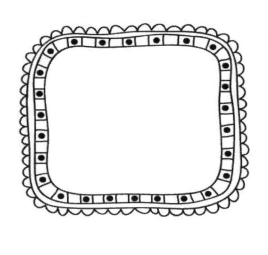

Date:_____

"For great things do not just
happen by impulse,
but are a succession of
small things linked together."
– Vincent Van Gogh

Date:_____

Date:_____

Date:_____

Date:_____

Date:_____

Date:_____

"It's not what happens to you, but how you react to it that matters."

— Epictetus

Date:_____

Date:_____

Date:_____

Date:_____

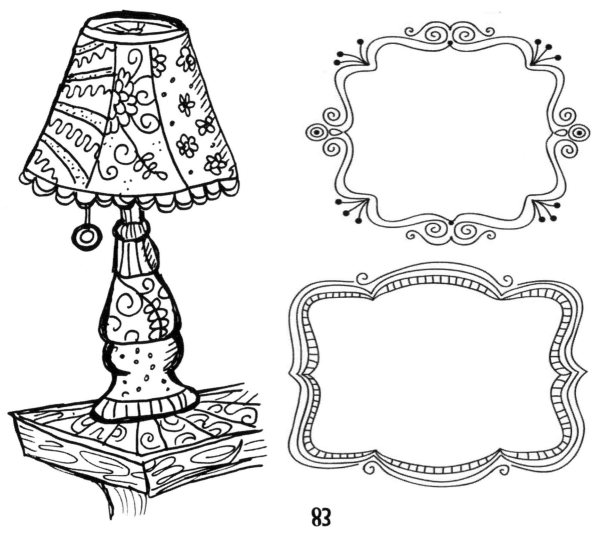

Date:_____

Date:_____

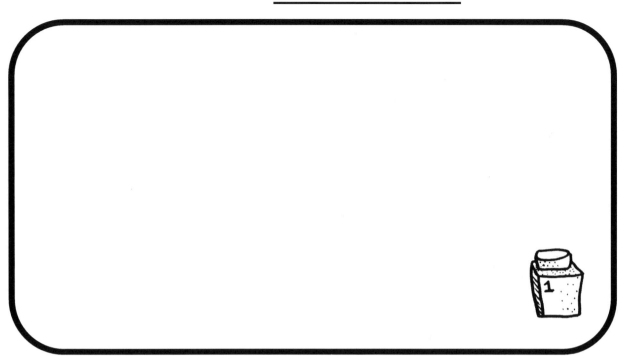

85

Date:_____

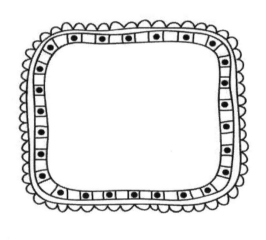

Date:_____

"What's fair will not always be equal."

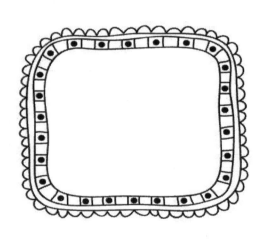

Date:_____

Date:_____

Date:_____

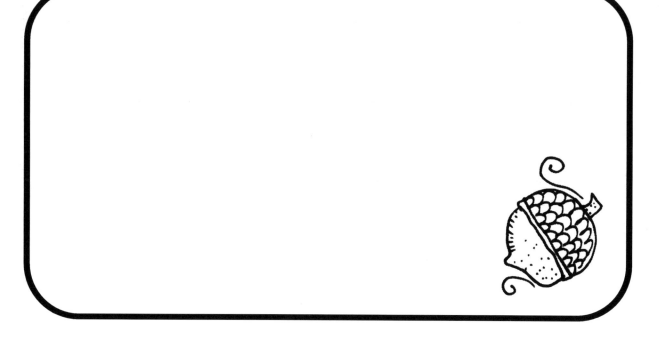

Date:_____

Date:_____

"Happiness doesn't result
from what we get,
but from what we give."

— Ben Carson

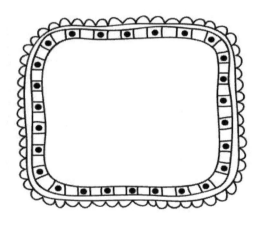

Date:_____

Date:_____

Date:_____

Animal Friends

Animal Friends

Date:_____

Date:_____

Date:_____

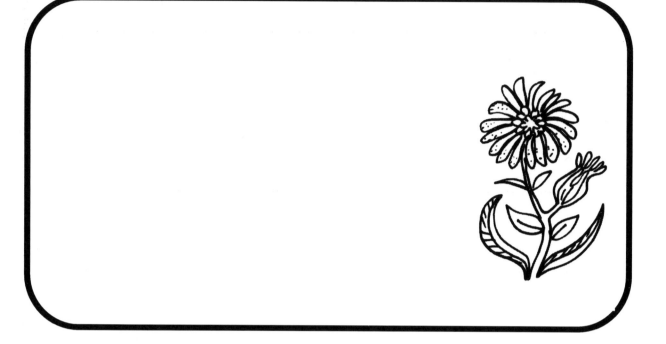

Date:_____

"There's the easy way
and the right way.
Which will you choose?"

Date:_____

Date:_____

Date:_____

Sailboat ★

Sailboat ★

Date:_____

Date:_____

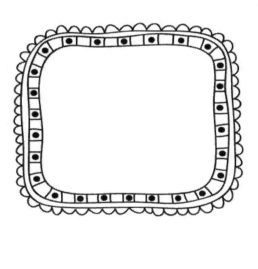

Date:_____

Date:_____

Date:_____

> "The world breaks everyone and afterward many are strong at the broken places."
>
> — Ernest Hemingway in "A Farewell to Arms"

Date:_____

Date:_____

Date:_____

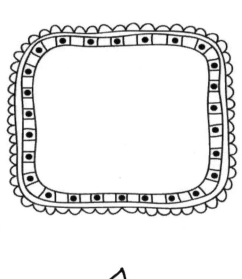

Date:_____

Date:_____

Date:_____

"Be truthful in what
you say and do."

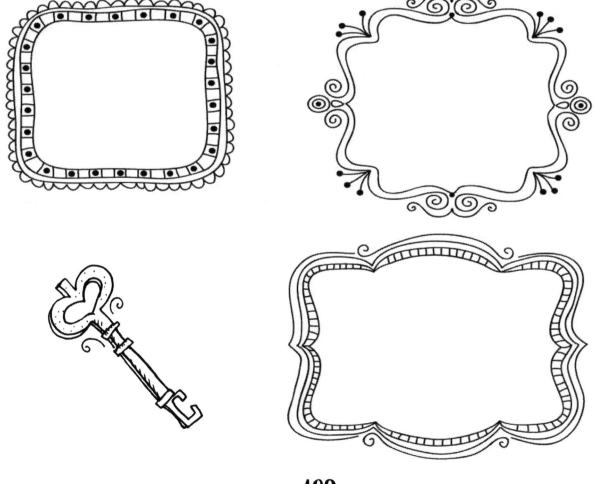

Date:_____

Date:_____

Date:_____

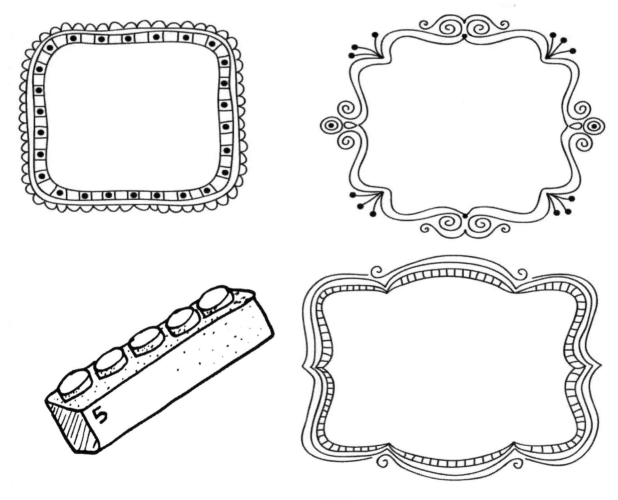

133

Date:_____

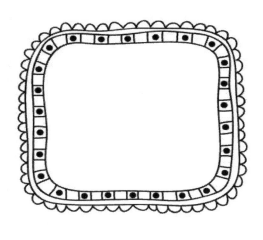

Date:_____

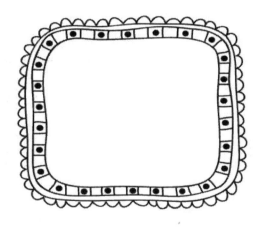

Date:_____

"You can do anything
you put your mind to.
Let no one make you feel
any less or like you can't."

Date:_____

Date:_____

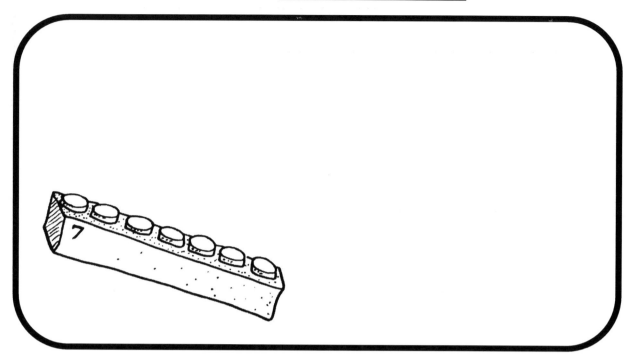

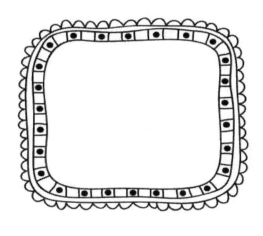

Date:_____

Date:_____

Date:_____

Date:_____

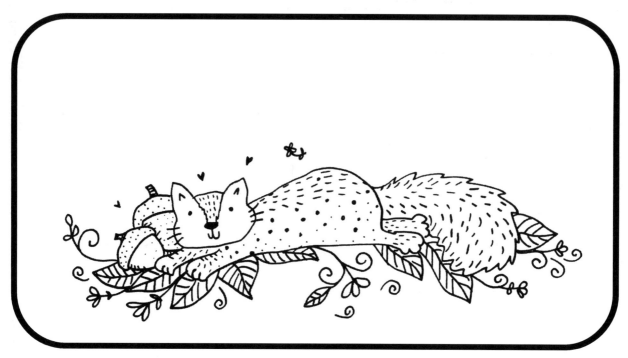

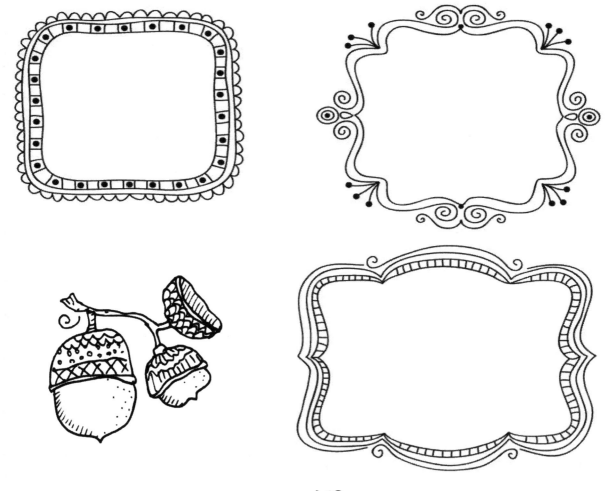

Date:_____

Date:_____

Date:_____

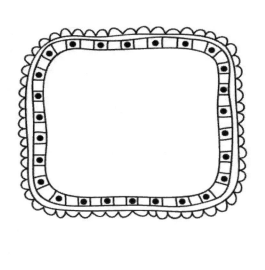

Date:_____

Date:_____

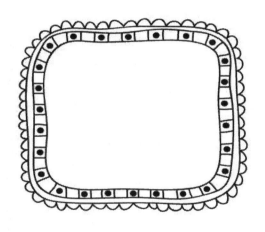

Date:_____

"Open your heart –
open it wide; someone is
standing outside."

– Mary Engelbreit

Date:_____

Date:_____

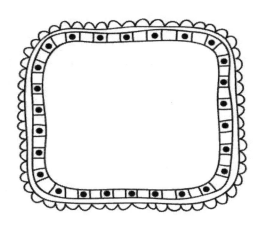

Date:_____

Date:_____

Date:_____

Date:_____

168

"If you judge people
you have no time
to love them."

– Mother Teresa

Date:_____

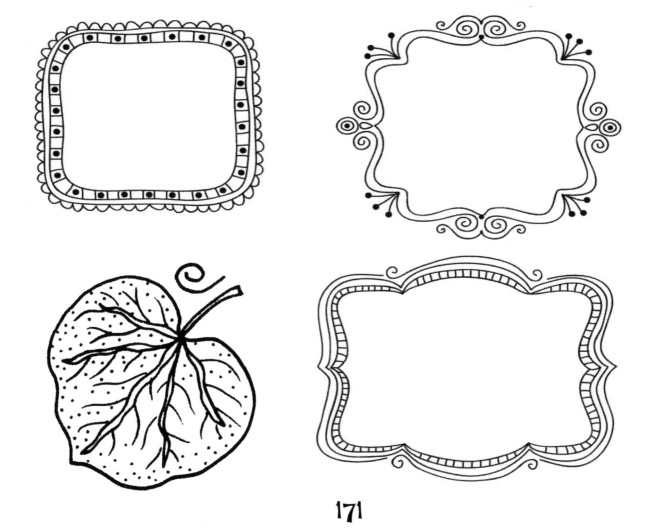

Date:_____

173

Date:_____

Date:_____

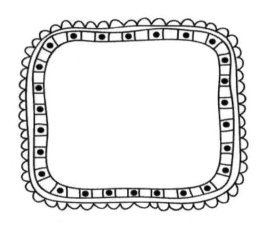

177

Date:_____

"Kind words are short and easy to speak, but their echoes are truly endless."

— Mother Teresa

Date:_____

THE Thinking TREE

PUBLISHING COMPANY

Sarah Janisse Brown